A COLLECTION OF POEMS

STEPHEN CALDWELL WRIGHT

OUT OF THE WAILING

A Christopherr-Burghardt Associates Publication
P. O. Box 520742
Longwood, Florida 32752-0742

The Printing Palace
Sanford, Florida

OUT OF THE WAILING

In the Storm,
Silence Intersects,
Never Releases.

After the Storm
Comes the Wailing.

After the Wailing
Comes the Storm.

STEPHEN CALDWELL WRIGHT

OUT OF THE WAILING

Page

FROM THE CITY

THE SOUTH, THE NORTH, THE NATION

Gray Moss
On Thin Limbs
Lies Still,
Clings
To Coarse,
Cracked Bark
Of Dying Tree.

NEW YORK'S EAST EIGHTIES

So Wonderful
They are in the Cities—
The older ones
In their new prime
Who, during or after
Their morning walks,
Purchase their Times
And settle
Their breakfast
Into place for lunch
With sometimes friends
But mostimes themselves.

Preserved
In wintry wrappings,
They drape herringbone
Across their shulders;
Twirl rainbow scarves
Around their necks;
Fish woolen mittens
In and out of their pockets.

A PATCH ALONG BROADWAY

In Empire City
On the water

Tall sunflowers
On slopes of clay
Winter-wither
In beds of rock

Know the haunt
Of but one Spring

HOUSES

City houses do not stand alone——

Lay claim to privacy,
Create individual arenas —

Without the sharing
Of their porches,
Stoops, and walks.

Fragrance of burning wood
Stiffens itself against rooftops;
Ashes whiten red-brown bricks,
Coat molding leaves.

Frost-wet stones belie
Recollected play places
On quiet streets,
Set to rage
By childish screams,
Rippling laughter —
Lost to roar of motors,
Not to drift of snails
Beneath wooden houses
Raised on cinder blocks
To cries of a different wild.

PRAYERS & PROMISES

MEN TALKING

These hours are without
The Children——

Without the Wives
Or the Friends
Of Long, Lasting Years.

The stray cat is sleeping
In the Farthest Corner
Beyond the trees.

The Dog is in the Neighbors' Yard
Listening to the shuffle
Of male tongues wagging.

The Roasting Burn
Of sizzling ribs,
Chicken, and burgers
Thickens the air.

The Fellas Sit in the Covering
           Of
           Oaks
           And
           Pines;

Laugh alive Off-Color Creations
           Of
           Lurid
           Past
           Impressions—

Locked within Little
           Less
           Than
           Over-Sensitive

Approaches to Painting of Themselves
           With
           Rugged
           Words,
           In
           Daring
           Strokes.

MY OTHER BROTHER

My other Brother
        Is more Properly attired
        To the brighter ranks,

And, though I do not Witness Myself
        In Suit and Tie,

I Glory his Spunk
        For ascension
        To the Hills
        The Capitols
        The Suburbs.
No Loss.   No Harm.
No Plantation.
No Reservation.

But —
I shall not
Be a brother in the Mix
        And twine of Contusion.

I like to raise
The windows at Dusk;

Hear the whispers
From the house next door;

See the homely children
Playing in the alleys
Under street lights;

Watch them plant their hopes
Against evening sky.

BEYOND RHYME

RAP is **not** RAPPING.
Rapping used to be a Delicate,
Long-Time composed
Sense of Serving
Selected Phrases
Into the Faces
Sweetly—
Of young Darlings
Or
Swiftly, Securely off the Faces
Of Bearded companions,
Busy from the Streets
Or
Strictly in the Games
Of playing the dozens,
Reconstructing Territory,
Or
Fighting without knife or Gun.

Now, rap is
"Approved" Rating
Of Minds Far Greater
Than the Media allows—
Minds trapped in the economy
Of Someone Else's Sanction.

So Pitiful, the World
Lost To
Many Definitions.

So much The Illusion;
So Vacant The Validity.

More Pitiful, The Seekers
Of Repackaged,
Hollywood Dreams —

Sold for the cost
Of Privacy
And Control.

RECONSTRUCTION
The Black Face in the Crowd, in the Wherever

You— the once/often outcast,
      Native Healer,
      Primitive Sorcerer,
      Quiet Griot—

You give Bounce, and Savvy
      To the quiet Others—
      Partners in Synthesis,
      Incessant Emulation.

You are the Scale by which Measures
      Are to be made into Law,
By which new cords are to be granted
      Entry to American "Bandstands."

Your ease of Language
      Colors their Blandness,
And such Wiggle you Instruct
      In their Waltzing.

Your inborne Posture
      Frames marvelous structuring,
Unquestionably Suited
      For Disclosure and Acclaim.

You embody Ancient Mathematics,
        Ivory and Coal Carvings
Of heroic contemplation,
        Smooth proportioning.

You engulf disconcerting Query
        Yet Remain the Sensor,
        Jutting into Constant
        Bewildering gaze

        As you slant
        Melodic phrases,
        Lively
        In mid-air.

You Gather from Fields of Yearning —
You Harvest among old Intentions.

Your Internal fire becomes

Your Salutation,
Your lasting Salute:

        You Always
        Your Face clean and shining
        Among white etcetera.

**TO YOUNG, UP & COMING AFRICAN AMERICAN REPUBLICANS
WHO TREASURE THE OPPORTUNISTIC VALUES OF THEIR WAYS**

You will build— eventually—
    A Barrier
Against this Oneness
    Which
Is the Keeping
    Of the Blessed Ones
Against whom you Likely
    Struggle—
For, despite your difficulty
    In abiding their faces,
They have become
The Initiates
    Who Gather At Water
To Find Release—
To Resist Capture;

To serve as buffer
Between your pride
And those other people's
Silent Hatred of you —

Their wonderful friends
Who are not
Like the others who continue
To Resist Compulsive Dilution.

FACADE BUILDERS

As skilled Whites replace old Blacks
In the new world order,
Convergence threatens
Further extinction,

And

Instead of whistling Dixie,
These brick-layers muscle up Smiles
　　　These Days
　　　When their Rarity
　　　Is Darkly Matched by Doormen,
　　　Janitors, and yardmen.

With Better-than-Average, Efficient
　　　Flick of wrist,
　　　Gallant Twitch
　　　And Turn of Trowel—
　　　They carefully stroke Slow,
　　　Gray-White cement
　　　Into Expressive Formation.

Within the corners of their private chatter,
　　　They heal themselves—
　　　Flesh glistening,
　　　Eyes sizzling
　　　In scorching glaze.

LIVING IN VERNACULAR

SHADOWS UNDER THE HANGING MOSS

They live to discuss Jesus,
How Good It Is To be Alive,
The price of beans,
The freshness of tomatoes,
The latest news
From down the street.

They do not image
Across their faces
The rush of Wall Street,
The Mid-East predicament
Nor the Great Grenada Farce
Except to say, to speak
The rumors of war,
The promises of famine.

They dance
Only in their minds,
And only then
To remembered cadence
Which keeps them

Coming back to
How Good It Is To Be Alive,

Coming back to continue
Bashing heads of Serpents,
Flicking Hungry Worms
From luscious greens,
Reciting the Commandments,
Singing and humming Beatitudes.

THE MOST DIFFERENCE
A rural grandmother watches her school-teacher daughter
and the daughter's husband

And *you* say you need
         a *pressed* Suit and Tie——
         And she is already *ready*
         To go, to visit the Center
         To be with The Proper Folk.

Your Staying In is **out**.
Enough.
Get up off your Assumptions and Prance,
Sanely to the closet of your Desires.

She says daily-in her-mind:
         I know no man cleaner,
                      better, finer.

You say: **I** am not the one.
         My Figure is not erect,
         Nor proper, nor so deftly
                  Inclined to mirror
                  Her Wonder,
                  Her Gracement.

She scoffs: I wish he **Would**.
You revel: I Can't.

You **Lie**.

SIGNALS

Two yardmen spreading mulch in the presence of small white kids

Said the darkest brother to the other:

You——with your curly head,
        your jive-eyed,
                polished face ——
You **Is Not** a King, Buddy.

You **Is** a man,
        As such, My Brother
        Not My Keeper-Understand?

(Reconsideration.)

(Retraction.)

(Stare.)

Hands High-Five
        Methodically
                To smug Conclusion.

They relent:

Now, *we* can go 'head on
          And do The Man's job—
                    Together—
But *You* **Is Not** No King, Buddy...

So don't be giving
Me no orders.

Drink your own beer.

Matter of fact,
Gimme some of yours.

'Member, what I say:
You is not no king, buddy.

So don't be buggin' out on me.

Real talk.

To the End.

Huh.

FANTASY FUSION
And the Black girls sang: See them fade, see the men fade away

So silly the observation/wonderment
        Over this stellar Whiteness
        Which looms above
        The common spectrum—
        Simple universal balance
        Of the color wheel.

Your skin is not *stellar*
        So coarse yet supple,
        So presently your own
        You sometimes forget
        To hug its abilities
        To fight hard against bleaching
        And lotioning and peeling.

Your ambitions clearly side-step
        Your Grandmother's Dreams,
        Your Grandfather's Visions;
        Cloud/Clog your efforts
        At penetration of Them
        Into Continual Generation.

Your Nightmares are the Usual Wonderings
        Of your Female Endeavors/Endearers
        Who Love you Still,
        Would love you *Anyway,*
        Without glamor of false pride—
        Certainly without marshmallow endearment.

So silly this fascination for transparency.

SOARING
A Black Man Speaks

In "the killing of Mockingbirds"
There is a poem
For Negro
        African-American
                        Males
Who do not read,
Do not walk through
        Documents of their tunneling
        Into the Center of Attraction;

Who do not look deeply
Beyond applause
        Within Concert walls,
        Inside sports arenas,
        Outside bright dance halls.

There is a rhythm to be found
        In the stretch
        Of Wild Wings
        Sounding the turmoil
        Of fighting To Be Free.
        Letting the Realness Begin.

There is honor in budding beyond prunning,
        In letting the treble of Spring
        Rattle unto green-ness
        Thin, brown limbs—
        Left For Dead
        So Many Winters.

STREET/SIDE

A Cool Cat Properly Capitulates

I bop the Scratch,
      Scan the scene—

My Lady
Counts My stride,
Got my time—
      Knows everywhere I Go,
          Done Been.

Don't need no smack—
      No Thank Ya, brother.

No Thank Ya, sister—
      Move along.   Quite set-already.

Oh, yeah.   We Cool.   You Cooler.
      Be Cool.   Now, get along, little buddy.

We don't need no zombies here.

Put it on hold—fellas!

Nawhhh...Ain't like crackin' no whip, brotherrrr.
      It ain't like that.

It's like-Respect-maaaann.

It ain't Friday for nothin'.
She 'pecting me.

M'Lady's Waiting.
      I gotta be clearin' out,
          Like now, like really now.
Hey, from the real side.   She's the True Authentic.

WHAT TIME IT IS

A Sister Laments:

Your
       Critical
           Choice
              Of words
Is An Art of Prowess,
      And You Handle Intricacies
      Easily Enough
To dispel Despair
      In A Thousand
Different Ways—
      Like Skinnin' the Cat,
      Copin' A Shine,
Being Real to the Shake,

Like Movin' Way From
      The Hot Spot when
The Deal Goes Down—

Cause, As You Say,
      Finally and Ultimately,
      From the "Hole,"

               "I Am The Hell Outta Here!"

She smiled,
But she was not smiling
Because he had got caught
Just as she said he would.

CHRISTINE REMEMBERS

She says:

And When You Were Good
                You Were Good

In Your Gentle Ways
On Your Gentler days

                When no Madness Clawed
                When no Sadness Mauled

Our Sleeping Formations
Warmly entwined.

JUSTINE REGRETS

After listening to his whining,
She slipped in between
His last sentence and the next one
Which she did not want to hear —
To say:

And then there is the one
About the "Negro"
Who froze to death
In his car
By turning his air-conditioner
As high as it would go —
To make his hair fly
Like that of the white boy
Beside him.

He started to say, but she kept talking:

And seeking further
To be content,
He nearly suffocated
While speeding
In his brand new convertible
When his hair still refused
To billow, to bounce—
To make light of itself.

Then, and only then,
Pausing at the edge of her patience,
She inquired:

"Are you sure you don't own a convertible?"

RESURGENCE

ABOUT (THE BUSINESS OF) BEING

When you have wrung
From this desert land
Of yours and ours
A ripeness for planting
Visions for reaping;

When you have wrought
Substantial whimsy,
Stirred it into quiet
Replacing of doubt
With catching of passion;

When you have finished
Tilling sharply the land,
Plowing richly the soil
For the New Ones
Willingly to rise;

When you have given,
When you have wrung,
When you have wrought,
Then will you have risen
To Passion's Fine Posing:

Then will you have
Upscaled Striving Others,
To Healthier Self-Portions —
To Higher Self-Rhythm.

SOJOURN
for Dr. Frederick S. Humphries
President, Florida A & M University

You Are For The World
To Know In giant stride
The wonders you, too, must grind
From Selective, Collective Minds—
True Deepness from Ages Past.

Within Your Suave Stature
Elevates Sure, Lasting
Pride and Prodding—
Larger than Selfdom.

You encase Promise—
Blending Orange and Green,
Gray, Yellow, White,
Red, and Black Faces...

Forging through,
Calmly assembling
Into a soothing cadence—
Like scattered clouds
Marching into formation
On late Sunday Afternoons.

REFLECTIONS FOR MOVIN' ON

When all of life was Song,
    In revelry the children gazed,
    In fantasy the children shuffled
    Their simplest thoughts,
    Their fondest dreams,
    Their greatest thrills
Against the silver screen,
Against technicolor skies.

When all of life was Song—
    No carefuless,
    No awfulness,
    No doubtfulness
With woes at their slightest,
Wonders at their brightest.

When all of life was Song,
They spun the hymns of zest,
    Laughed through mockery
    Of gangster heroes,
    White hats, white horses.

These things, these things and more
When all of life was Song.

PRAISE FOR BUSTER
for N.R.F

As you chart my memory,
You construct the idea of waltzing;

When you swing, when you sway
With the notes from the trumpet,
And the trumpeter stands,
Swoons in echo to the horns—
The strings begin vibrating,
Begin cutting through,
Becalming your chordal gaze.

Etched tight and blade-quick,
The treble of your motions
Traces pulsations of the flesh—
Resolves into sombre notes
Of almost unspoken-ness.

Your waltzing enacts crescendo,
Stirs silence into fury,
Gives rise to pauses:
Creates a mural—
Lasting, somnolent.

SHOUT
First Sunday Morning In The New Year

This Song Is Not
Dedicated to the Achieving Few
Who have arrived——
On the blood and bones and marrow
Of striving others before them——

Arrived beyond recognition
Of still-striving
Pre-schoolers;
Secondary warriors;
Displaced/misplaced
Mothers and fathers;
Wearily busy
And busier becoming
Uncles and grandfathers,
Grandmothers, and aunts.

This Song Is Not Lined
To melody of new black faces
Stretching beyond grimace
Into marshmallow comfort
Of the Republican Zone;
Onto hollow Horizon
Of Democratic vistas.

This Is Not Your Song.

This Is Not The Song
For intellectual Zombies,
Soothed to "safe" contradiction
Of their paths and themselves.

This Can Not Be A Song
For chosen prescribers,
Newly tarred and soon enough
To be feathered—

Who advance happily
Creative confusion
Of "Conservative" versus "Liberal";

Who, having reached
Surburban Sufficiency,
Have lost their willingness,
Lost their determination
To be Thin in Hungry Times.

This Song Is Not Dedicated To Those
Who have Fallen To Formulae:
This can not be their lullaby.

Song Must Become Sermon
To Muster Their Salvation.

This Song
Is For The Other Young and Old,

All Who Are

Sturdy in Seeking;
Hugging of Truth;
Loving of Themselves.

To These Is This Song Sung.

OUT OF THE WAILING

I Hold A Lust To See People
See them moving,
Waltzing and bopping

Moving and Doing Things
Natural to their Souls

Like Singing Opera
Like Dancing Ballet
Like Playing Joplin

Waltzing, Bopping
Doing the Rag

Naturally to their Souls

Moving and Doing Things
Uplifting and Renewing

Like Blooming and Becoming

Like Popping Blues
Like Hopping Reggae
Like Shouting Spirituals
Like Humming Hymns
Like Clicking Tap...

I Hold A Lust To See People
To See My People
In Holy Orchestration:

"From Pyramids
To Skyscrapers"*

From cutting celery
To Sweeping Floors

From Office Windows
To Factory Doors

From Mango Groves
To Shipping decks

From Stylish Mansions
To Shotgun Houses

I Hold A Lust To see My People

See Them Moving
Moving and Doing

Doing Things Natural

Like Surviving —
High-Stepping Style,
With Souls Intact

Like Looking
In The Mirror
And Smiling Back.

***"From pyramids to skyscrapers"**
**Words of Dr. Richard K. Dozier, Professor of Architecture at Florida A
& M University, who also said: "W. E. B. DuBois wrote books, and
Booker T. Washington trained the people who built the libraries that
housed the books."**

MONOLOGUES

DISPENSATION

You Disappoint Me——
     Sure, and Finely I regret
     Yet, Finely I remember
Your gift of Gwendolyn's Poetry
Recorded live, in her Voice

     Her early Voice——
Now little more framed in deeper echo——
That girlish wonder
     Youthful Womanhood,
Lilting, strength-stretched
     to tender
       reeling,
     melodious constancy.

This Voice-
     Hers, not yours, is the Saving
     of Your Soul—— Our Would Have Been
     Stronger Than Ever Friendship.

I had but forgot this offering,
     Now a testament
       to your relishing
         of things Shown Pure ——

Her Voice Dancing in the Light
     against and among
     rare books,
     painted screens,
     selected photographs,
     porcelain and glass,
     paper boxes,
     wooden latches,
     key chains,
     discarded letters
     and others—

     Remnants from
     Relationships,
     Arrangements,
     Departures...

This Voice —
     Hers, not yours,
     Is the Saving
     Of Your Soul —

Her Voice Still Dancing —
     Her Voice Still Singing
Where you once were Revered,
     Often Walked, Lived.

STEPHEN'S ODE

You Touched the Surface of My Heart,
And I want you to know it.

Just in case you did not think
I saw through your eyes
The power of your Dreams,
The joy and splatter of your touch...

Perhaps, by chance or choice inpression,
You did not think I was fully there,
Was yours for the asking and the keeping;

Just in case you did not notice
The flame and fervor of my embrace,
The gentle release of my fears...

Perhaps, by choice or chance impression,
I did not Dance to your realizations,
Did not the music of your mind make...

Say I, still-Smiling in Dare:

You Touched the Surface of My Heart,
And I want you to know it.

Just in case, Perhaps, by Chance,
You Remembered but forgot
Our Breaking of Day from Night,
The turn of Darkness to Light,

Just in case ——
You Touched the Surface of My Heart
And I want you to know it.

Perhaps, by Chance or Choice,
You May Sing This in Your Sleep.